Contents

Chapter 1

WHAT IS A POLITICAL MAP?

Imagine you are trying to find buried treasure. You have a map that leads the way. An *X* on the map marks the spot of the treasure. You don't see an *X* on the ground, of course. But thanks to the map, you know exactly where to dig.

Maps can show us many things about a place. What does this map show?

Maps can serve many purposes. A map may show the location of treasure. It may show natural features on Earth, such as mountains and deserts.

A map may show places that have been created by people. It may show the borders that separate these places. These borders aren't features of the land, the way mountains or deserts are. They are imaginary, like the *X* on the treasure map. A map that shows human places and their borders is called a political map.

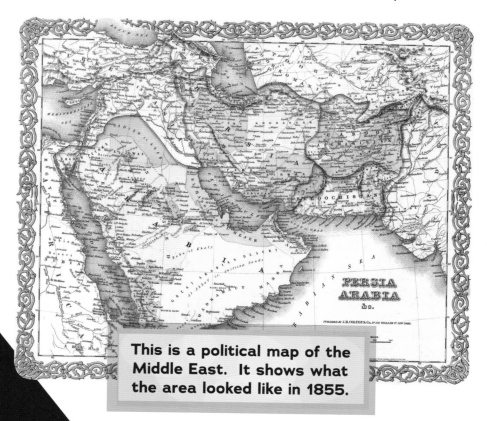

This is a political map of the Middle East. It shows what the area looked like in 1855.

A political map may show different countries and their capitals. It may show states, provinces, counties, cities, and other important places. Any place that was created by people might appear on a political map.

A map like this one may be hanging in your classroom. Maps that show states are political maps.

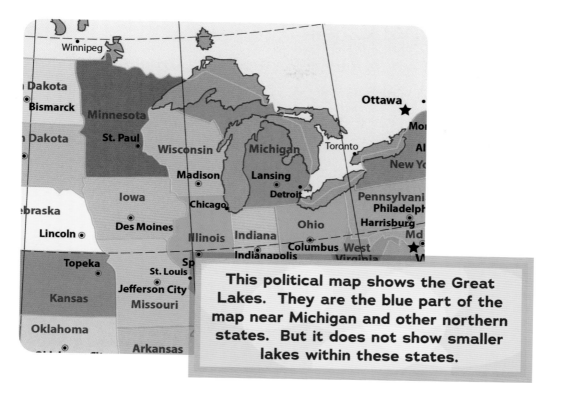

This political map shows the Great Lakes. They are the blue part of the map near Michigan and other northern states. But it does not show smaller lakes within these states.

No single map can show everything. For this reason, cartographers (people who make maps) choose what places they want to emphasize. They include only the features that will be important to people using the map.

A political map may show important bodies of water, such as rivers and lakes. But you probably will not see mountains or deserts on a political map. You'll mostly just see human-made things.

Globes vs. Political Maps

If you wanted to see all the countries on Earth, you could look at a globe. A globe is a tiny model of Earth. It shows the true shape of Earth—a sphere. A globe can show you all the countries on the planet, but it can show you only part of Earth at one time. If you want to see countries on the other side of the world, you have to turn the globe.

GLOBES SHOW ALL SEVEN CONTINENTS, BUT YOU MUST TURN THE GLOBE TO SEE THEM.

Maps through History

People have been making maps for thousands of years. In ancient times, they painted or carved maps of their surroundings on rock or clay. As civilization grew, mapmakers drew maps of distant lands based on reports and drawings from explorers and travelers. Modern cartographers rely on aerial and satellite photography to map the world. They draw maps by putting together these photographs like puzzle pieces.

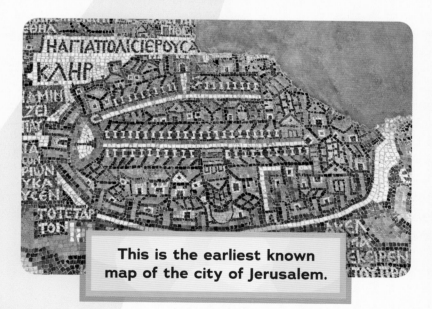

This is the earliest known map of the city of Jerusalem.

If you want to see all the countries of the world at once, you will have to look at a political map. A political map of the entire Earth shows all the countries of the world. A political map may show the entire Earth or any part of Earth. It may show many countries or just one country. Or it may show just one state, such as the state where you live.

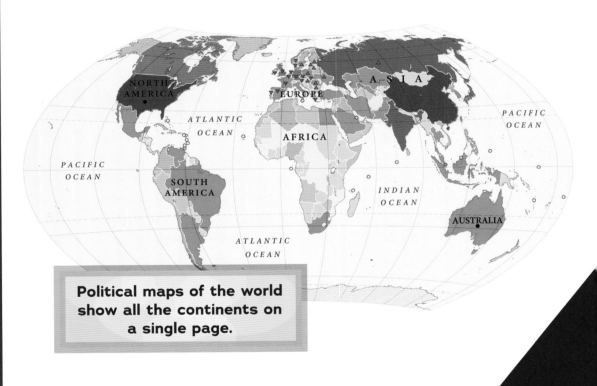

Political maps of the world show all the continents on a single page.

Chapter 2

WHAT'S ON A POLITICAL MAP?

Political maps use a special language. It includes symbols, names, numbers, lines, and colors. You can learn how to read this language. Political maps use symbols that are simple and easy to understand. The meaning of these symbols is shown in a legend, or key. The legend is usually in a box near a corner of the map.

The box in the right-hand corner of this map helps you understand the symbols on the map. What is this guide to the map's symbols called?

Dots and Stars

Dots on a political map often stand for cities and towns. Sometimes the dots are the same size. Sometimes they are different sizes. Look at the legend to understand the meaning of different-sized dots. Large dots may show large cities with lots of people. Small dots may show smaller cities and towns.

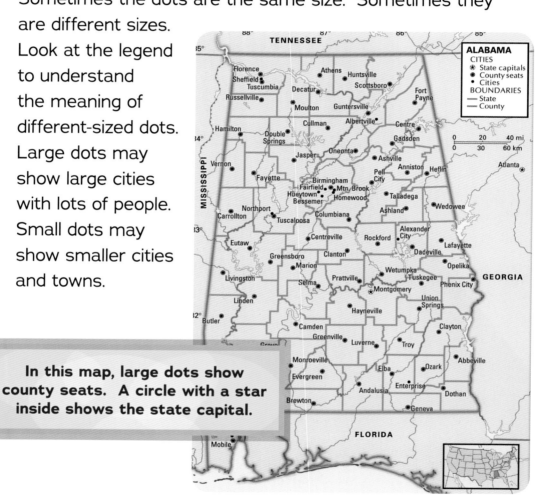

In this map, large dots show county seats. A circle with a star inside shows the state capital.

Many maps use a star inside a circle to show capitals. Others use dots inside circles. A map may use different symbols for the capital of a country versus the capital of a state. For example, a political map of the United States might have one symbol for Washington, DC (the nation's capital) and a different symbol for the capital of a state.

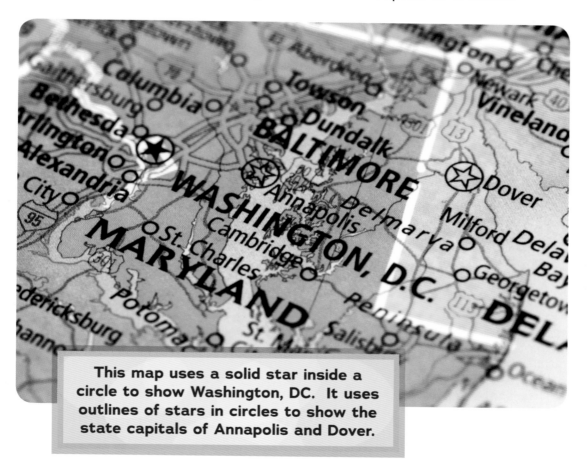

This map uses a solid star inside a circle to show Washington, DC. It uses outlines of stars in circles to show the state capitals of Annapolis and Dover.

Lettering

Mapmakers use different types of lettering to identify different features. They might use different fonts, styles, sizes, and colors. The name of a country may be shown in capital letters. The name of a capital city may be shown in bold letters. The names of other cities may be shown in lowercase letters.

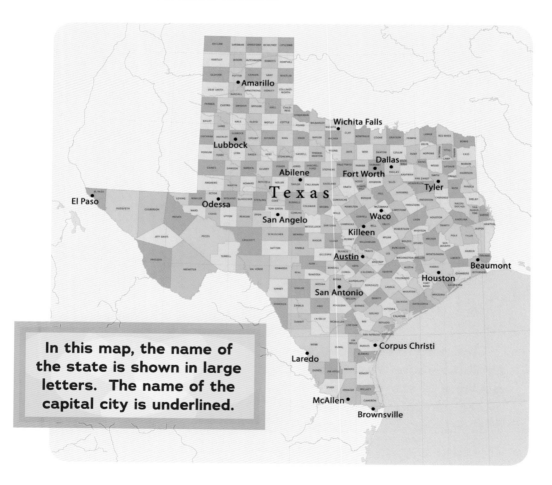

In this map, the name of the state is shown in large letters. The name of the capital city is underlined.

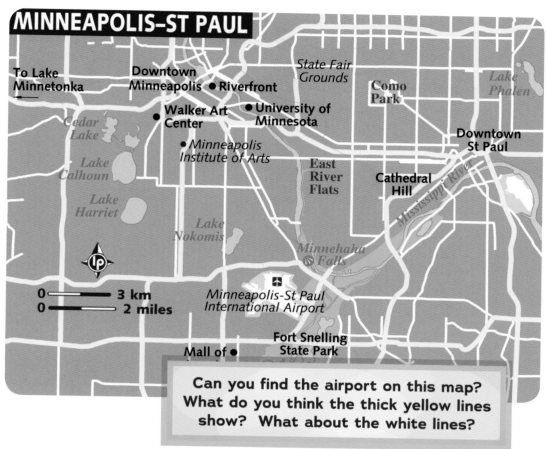

MINNEAPOLIS-ST PAUL

To Lake Minnetonka

Downtown Minneapolis • Riverfront

State Fair Grounds

Como Park

Lake Phalen

Cedar Lake

Walker Art Center

• University of Minnesota

• Minneapolis Institute of Arts

Downtown St Paul

Lake Calhoun

East River Flats

Cathedral Hill

Mississippi River

Lake Harriet

Lake Nokomis

Minnehaha Falls

0 — 3 km
0 — 2 miles

Minneapolis-St Paul International Airport

Mall of •

Fort Snelling State Park

Can you find the airport on this map? What do you think the thick yellow lines show? What about the white lines?

Lines

Some political maps show highways, roads, and railroads. Lines stand for highways and roads. The thickest lines show the biggest roads. Crossed lines are used for railroads. They look like railroad tracks. An airport may be shown with an airplane symbol.

Lines also show borders between countries, provinces, and states. Some borders are shown with a straight line. Others are shown with a curvy line. Borders shown with curvy lines are usually those that follow physical features of the land. These might include coastlines, rivers, or the top of a mountain range.

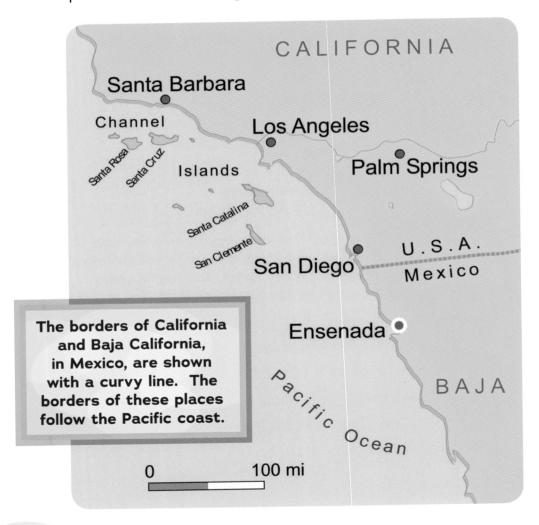

CALIFORNIA

Santa Barbara

Channel

Santa Rosa

Santa Cruz

Islands

Los Angeles

Palm Springs

Santa Catalina

San Clemente

San Diego

U.S.A.

Mexico

The borders of California and Baja California, in Mexico, are shown with a curvy line. The borders of these places follow the Pacific coast.

Ensenada

BAJA

Pacific Ocean

0   100 mi

Colors

Some political maps contain many bright colors. The colors make it easy to see the borders between countries, states, or counties. The same color may be used more than once on a map. But the same colors are never used right next to each other. This helps map users tell different countries, states, or counties apart.

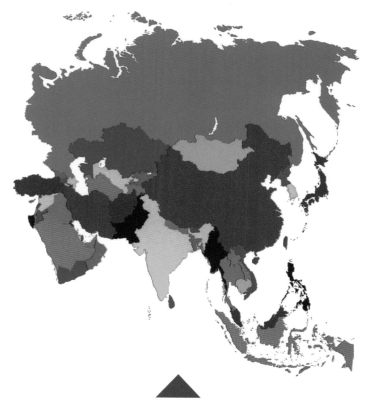

THIS MAP OF ASIA SHOWS THE CONTINENT'S COUNTRIES IN DIFFERENT COLORS.

The Four-Color Theorem

Mathematics has a famous rule that mapmakers use. It is called the four-color theorem. Imagine a map with many countries. Four colors are enough to color the map so that no two countries bordering each other have the same color. You can use a lot more colors on your map, but four is all you will ever need.

Four colors are all you need to add color to a map!

Only north is labeled on this map's compass rose. East is right, and west is left. To help you remember this, just remember this sentence: Never Eat Soggy Waffles!

Compass Rose

A political map shows direction. It shows which way is north, south, east, and west. When you are walking around outside, a compass can show you which direction you are going. The magnetic needle of a compass always points north. On a political map, a compass rose shows direction. A compass rose looks and works much like a compass. It shows you which way is north, south, east, and west on a map.

Scale

A political map also shows distances. A political map is always drawn smaller than the actual place it represents. At the bottom of many maps, you will see something that looks like a ruler. It is a tool known as the scale. Scales can be shown in different ways, but those that look like rulers are the most common kind. A scale helps you understand distances on the map. The scale shows that a certain distance on the map stands for a certain distance on Earth.

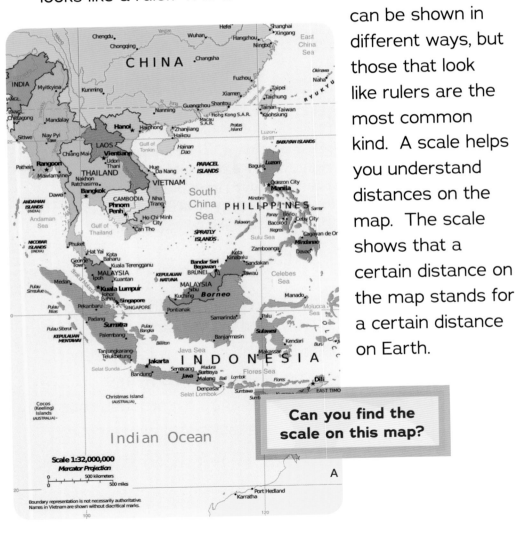

Can you find the scale on this map?

Latitude and Longitude

Political maps sometimes have lines running up and down and side to side. The up-and-down lines run north and south. The side-to-side lines run east and west.

THIS MAP FROM LONG AGO HAS LINES RUNNING UP AND DOWN AND SIDE TO SIDE.

The north-and-south lines on a political map are called longitude lines. The east-and-west lines are called latitude lines. The latitude line in the middle of Earth is called the equator. It divides the world into north and south. The map below shows where the equator passes through Brazil. What other countries does the equator pass through on this map?

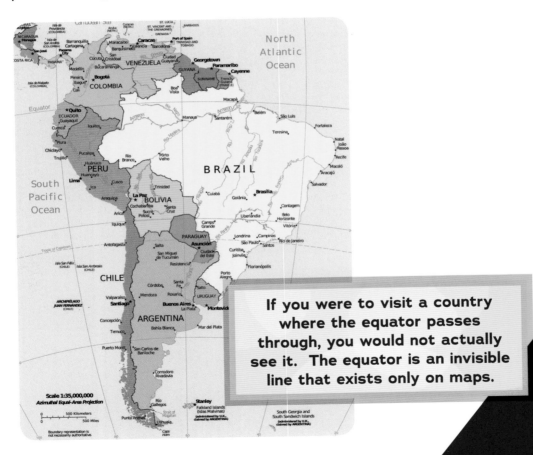

If you were to visit a country where the equator passes through, you would not actually see it. The equator is an invisible line that exists only on maps.

Chapter 3

HOW DO YOU USE A POLITICAL MAP?

Using a political map means knowing how to use its tools. To find out how far it is from one place to another, you use the scale.

On scales that look like rulers, miles and kilometers are often marked. To find the distance between two cities, line up the edge of a sheet of paper between them and make a mark at each city. Then move the paper to the scale. Line up one mark with the zero and read the distance opposite the other mark.

This map has a scale. What can you find out using a scale?

Sometimes scale is given in words. If the scale says "1 inch (2.5 centimeters) equals 10 miles (16 kilometers)," this means that 1 inch on the map equals 10 miles on the ground. To find the distance between two cities, use a ruler to measure the distance between them in inches. Then multiply the inches by 10 to get the number of miles.

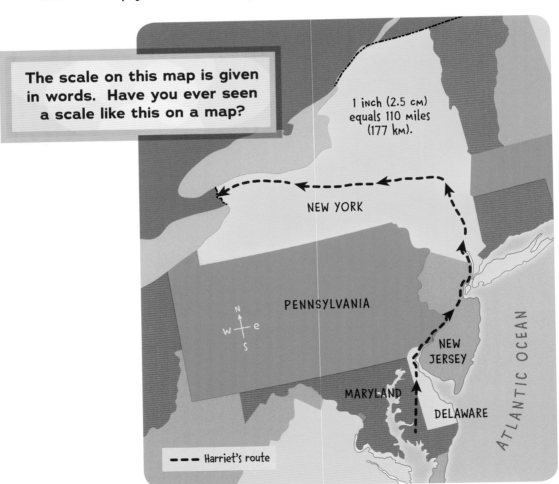

The scale on this map is given in words. Have you ever seen a scale like this on a map?

1 inch (2.5 cm) equals 110 miles (177 km).

NEW YORK

PENNSYLVANIA

N
W   e
S

NEW JERSEY

MARYLAND

DELAWARE

ATLANTIC OCEAN

--- Harriet's route

Scale is sometimes given as a ratio or a fraction, such as 1:1,000,000. In the ratio, the first number is always 1. This is a distance on the map, like 1 inch.

The second number shows the actual distance on Earth. It is different for each map. A scale of 1:1,000,000 means that 1 inch on the map represents 1,000,000 inches (2,540,000 cm), or 15.8 miles (25.4 km), on the ground. To find the distance on a map that uses this kind of scale, measure the distance between two cities. Then multiply the inches by 1,000,000 to get the distance in inches on land. You can convert inches to miles using this formula: 1 mile (1.609 km) equals 63,360 inches (160,934 cm).

1:800,000

The scale on this map is given as a ratio. Have you seen a scale like this?

Finding Places

To use a political map to find a particular place on Earth, you can use the latitude and longitude lines. Latitude lines are measured from the equator. Distances between the lines are measured in degrees. The equator is 0 degrees. The next line above it is 10 degrees north. The next one above that is 20 degrees north, and so on. The lines continue to the North Pole, which is 90 degrees north.

The lines below the equator work the same way. The line directly below the equator is 10 degrees south. The next one down is 20 degrees south. The lines continue in this way until they reach the South Pole, which is 90 degrees south.

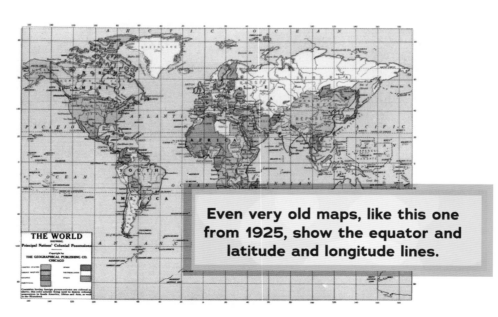

Even very old maps, like this one from 1925, show the equator and latitude and longitude lines.

A map's longitude lines are measured from the prime meridian. This imaginary line runs through Greenwich, England. The prime meridian is 0 degrees. The other longitudes are measured in degrees going east or west. There are 180 longitude lines east of the prime meridian and 180 longitude lines west of the prime meridian.

This line in Greenwich, England, symbolizes the prime meridian line.

To use latitude and longitude lines to find a place on a map, look up the latitude and longitude of the place. You can do this through a web search, or a librarian can help you find a resource that contains this information. It is very important to note whether the longitude is east or west. An address of 35 degrees north latitude and 115 degrees west longitude is in California. But an address with the same latitude and a longitude of 115 degrees east is across the world in China!

Whether you find California (left) or China (right) on a map depends on knowing whether the longitude is east or west.

IT'S REWARDING TO KNOW HOW TO USE A MAP TO FIND PLACES IN THE WORLD!

Once you have the latitude and longitude, go to a political map. Find the lines that mark the place's latitude and longitude. Follow the lines to the spot where they meet. You've found your place on the map!

Learning about States

You can also use a political map to learn about US states. A political map of the United States can show you where each state is. You can check how large each state is on the map to get an idea of how big the states are compared to one another. In addition, you can see which states border one another and which border other countries. You can learn the capitals of all the states too, as well as the names of many large cities.

You can learn a lot by studying a US map.

Learning about Countries

Another thing political maps are good for is learning about other countries. For instance, if you were doing a report on Germany, you could look at a political map of Europe. You can see where Germany is located and the countries it borders. You can see whether it is next to an ocean. You can learn the name of its capital as well as the names of other important cities.

What countries does Germany border? What is its capital?

Did You Know?

In ancient times, world maps were incomplete. Mapmakers relied on drawings and reports from explorers and travelers. If a place hadn't been explored yet, it did not make it onto the map. The first map showing the whole world was created in 1507 after Christopher Columbus and other explorers sailed around the world.

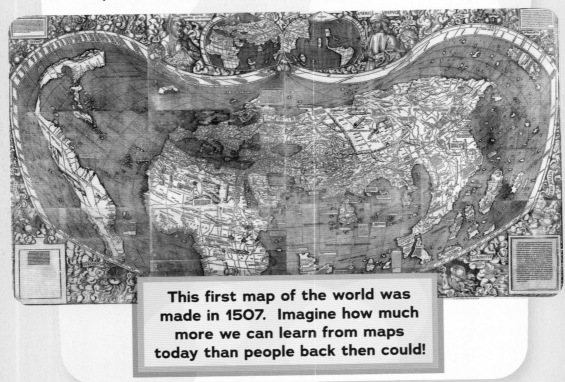

This first map of the world was made in 1507. Imagine how much more we can learn from maps today than people back then could!

Chapter 4

ARE YOU A POLITICAL MAP WHIZ?

Now that you've learned about political maps, it's time to put your knowledge to use! Imagine you live in North Dakota. You've always wanted to visit the nearby states. This summer, you heard good news. Your grandpa is taking you and your cousins on a road trip. You'll go to all the states that border your state. Which states will you visit?

Take a close look at this map. Can you use it to name the states you'd visit on your imaginary road trip?

Your grandpa said he wants to end the trip by taking you and your cousins fishing. You'll be heading north to Lake Manitoba, where your grandpa used to go fishing when he was young. Where is this lake? Is it in the United States?

What other lake is near Lake Manitoba?

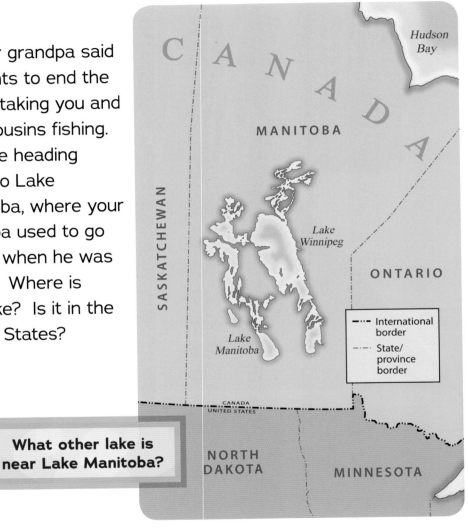

What happens if you get tired of fishing? You don't need to worry. Your grandpa says that you can visit a place nearby. He says the location is near 50 degrees north latitude and 100 degrees west longitude. What place do you think he's talking about?

You can find out on the Internet about things to do in a town you might be visiting.

What would you most like to learn from a political map?

You Did It!

Congratulations! You've just used a political map. Political maps help you explore your world and learn about places that people have created. They show information about cities, counties, states, provinces, and countries. They can also help you understand how places have changed over time. How else can you use a political map?

Fun Facts

- There are more than 190 countries on Earth. The newest is South Sudan in Africa. It became a country in 2011.

- The 0 degree longitude is the starting point for measuring east and west, but mapmakers did not always agree where to put it. Mapmakers from different countries put it through their own capital cities. In 1884, mapmakers agreed to put the prime meridian through Greenwich, England.

- At night, the prime meridian is marked by a laser beam that shoots north from the Royal Observatory in Greenwich, England. The laser can be seen for more than 36 miles (58 km)!

Glossary

border: a boundary of a country or state

cartographer: a person who makes maps

compass rose: a circle showing the directions of north, south, east, and west on a map

equator: an imaginary circle around Earth halfway between the North Pole and the South Pole

latitude: a distance north or south of the equator measured in degrees

legend: an explanatory list of symbols on a map. Legends are also called keys.

longitude: a distance east or west measured in degrees of the prime meridian

prime meridian: the 0-degree longitude that runs through Greenwich, England

scale: a tool that explains the size of a map compared to the actual place it represents

sphere: a ball-shaped object

LERNER
SOURCE™

Expand learning beyond the printed book. Download free, complementary educational resources for this book from our website, www.lerneresource.com.

Learn More about Political Maps

Books

Hirsch, Rebecca E. *What's Great about Washington, DC?* Minneapolis: Lerner Publications, 2015. Take a fun-filled tour of the United States' capital, complete with maps and interesting facts.

Isaacs, Sally Senzell. *Ultimate Globetrotting World Atlas.* Washington, DC: National Geographic Society, 2014. Learn fascinating information about the countries of the world with fun facts, political maps, and games.

Rajczak, Kristen. *Latitude and Longitude.* New York: Gareth Stevens, 2015. Check out this book to learn more about latitude and longitude.

Websites

Enchanted Learning: World Geography
http://www.enchantedlearning.com/geography
Check out this collection of maps, printouts, flags, and more from Enchanted Learning.

50 States
http://www.50states.com
This site has fun facts about the fifty states and plenty of maps you can print.

Math Is Fun: Coloring—the Four Color Theorem
http://www.mathsisfun.com/activity/coloring.html
Investigate the four-color theorem with coloring activities and puzzles at the Math Is Fun website.

Index

Photo Acknowledgments

The images in this book are used with the permission of: © iStockphoto.com/VladSt, p. 4; G. W. Colton/Wikimedia Commons, p. 5; © Sasa1867/Deposit Photos, pp. 6, 7; © iStockphoto.com/Christopher Futcher, pp. 8, 30; © iStockphoto.com/WitR, p. 9; © Dorling Kindersley/Getty Images, p. 10; © Encyclopaedia Britannica/Universal Images Group Limited/Alamy, pp. 11, 12; © iStockphoto.com/omersukrugoksu, p. 13; © iStockphoto.com/FrankRamspott, p. 14; © Lonely Planet/Getty Images, p. 15; © MAPS.com/Corbis, p. 16; © Volina/Deposit Photos, p. 17; © iStockphoto.com/Zmiy, p. 18; © Mike Kowalski/Illustration Works/Getty Images, p. 19; © JRTBurr/Deposit Photos, pp. 20, 22; © Historic Map Works LLC/Getty Images, pp. 21, 26; © iStockphoto.com/PeterHermesFurian, p. 23; © Laura Westlund/Independent Picture Service, pp. 24, 25, 34, 35; © Steve Vidler/SuperStock, p. 27; © iStockphoto.com/stevegeer, p. 28 (left); © iStockphoto.com/hapiphoto, p. 28; © Blend Images/SuperStock, p. 29; © iStockphoto.com/ilynx_v, p. 31; Library of Congress Geography and Map Division, p. 32; © olinchuk/Deposit Photos, p. 33; © iStockphoto.com/STEEX, p. 36.

Front cover: © Laura Westlund/Independent Picture Service.

Main body text set in Adrianna Regular 14/20
Typeface provided by Chank